BEinG

[Definition]
G & J Entertainment LLC 2016

[def-uh-nish-uh n]

[def-uh-nish-uh n]

Acknowledgments

I would like to thank my family first. My mother who has always been a major motivator and inspiration in my journeys of life. My father who through his experiences and through lessons of persistence, like my mother, has never let me give up. My brothers, for they have been sources of knowledge my entire life. My stepmother, who like my mother, has fully supported me and my endeavors since I began this journey. I love you all.

I would like to thank my best friend and fraternity brother John. Without his guidance and his encouragement, [Definition] may not exist. It was in my time of need that he helped me realize that I was more than what I thought I was. I love you my brother, IZ.

I would like to thank my friend Haymaker for his guidance and wisdom on my path to being who I am supposed to be. The long talks and lessons we shared will remain with me for a lifetime. I appreciate your taking me under your wing.

I would finally like to thank Alex for coming with me on this journey and lending his artistic ability to enhance my poetry. We made it my friend...

-Outlaw G

Thanks to my parents for providing a stable life, and emotional support.

I owe much to Tim and Don for always being there and encouraging me to grow as a person and an artist. I love you, Tim.

Finally, thanks to G for the pleasure of working together on BEinG and the projects to come.

-Alex

[def-uh-nish-uh n]

BEinG

- THE WEIGHT

- THE LEVEE

- SIX SIDED DIE

- SELF-REFLECTION

- PUT BACK TOGETHER

- DUALITY OF MAN (B E IN G)

- MARIGOLD

- 21

- DRIVE

- ENLIGHTENMENT

- FROM A PLACE

- I CARE G

[def-uh-nish-uh n]

THE WEIGHT

"The Weight" is a description of life and how it can hold an individual down. Life, at times, can be too much for some to bare. It is this weight that can keep a person trapped and helpless. "The Weight" is also to remind you that when the world is on your chest, you just need to push to get it off. Always remember that the weight will come back. The key is to keep pushing to make yourself stronger and more accustomed to life and its pitfalls. Never stop pushing to be who you are, and who you are supposed to be. Harness the strength that lies deep inside yourself.

-Outlaw G

[def-uh-nish-uh n]

THE WEIGHT

With the weight of the world on your chest,
You must get it off…
Because the cost of life,
In this life,
Won't let you rest,

Not at all…

In peace…

You can't cease and desist,
The fire and desire inside…
It's why you exist…
The more you worry,
The more your mind generates ire,
Don't retire…
Don't expire…
Not to the wills of the world,
Hold your head higher…

Chest out,
Chin up,
Look towards the horizon…
Start eyeing what is depraving,
Start defying what is depriving…

Holding you not to move,
Push with all you have,
Do what you must do…

In truth…

Your heart is your strength,
And when you let,
Some one…
Some thing…
Take that away…
You allow yourself to become easy prey,
For the world to prey on you,

[def-uh-nish-uh n]

It will keep you this way…
Flat backed on the bench you try to push,
But stuck holding the grip…

Failing… Falling…

But don't stop pushing…

You have one of two options…
When the world is on your chest,
Push it off,
Or let it lay you to rest…

Your life is on you,
You have no one to spot you…
If you can't push it off,
You allow life to stop you…

It will stop you,
If you do not harness your strength…
It is up to you to push past this weight…

Push it up… Lock it out…
Finish this rep…
One down… Nine to go…
Never settle… Never rest…

Push On…

[def-uh-nish-uh n]

THE LEVEE

"When the The Levee Breaks" is a song by the band Led Zeppelin and is the main influence of this piece. Sometimes in life we find ourselves under immense pressure from our friends, family, workplace, and ultimately ourselves. We also face the evils of life. There are people of the world who aim to inflict harm on you and others. "The Levee" represents these negative factors. The key in this case is to not let life's pressures and harmful people keep you from reaching your full potential. Instead, it is up to you to break through these obstacles or break "The Levee" to truly define yourself. When you have finally had enough of life's pressures and pain, you start to realize you have more to live for. Your true self is the water that is waiting and being held back by "The Levee."
Break through it...

-Outlaw G

[def-uh-nish-uh n]

THE LEVEE

If this pain keeps flowing,
The levee is going to break...

If this pain keeps growing,
The levee is going to break...

When it breaks,
Make no mistake,
That those who oppose you,
Have sealed their own fate...

The predators of this world prey on the weak,
Your bones,
Your flesh,
They will grind in their teeth...

But you can move mountains,
With every word you speak,
Against these predators,
You can make them all flee...

Speak free...

Live free...

Bring fear to those cowards,
Be the master of your destiny,
Let no evil devour...
When the levee breaks,
All of your enemies will be showered,
With the sight of your light,
And your words of immense power...

Empower yourself...

For your levee is soon to break,

It's just another step on this path that you pave...

[def-uh-nish-uh n]

Some day…

Some day soon,
You too will face the predators of life,
They have a will to consume,

Everything around you…

Everything about you…

They will make you lose who you are,
They will chew you up and spit you out,
Leaving you only with scars,
Of who you were,
They will leave you as a shell,
A hollowed out being,

Trapped between heaven and hell…

But when the levee breaks,
You will hear victory bells,
For the time has arrived,
Your heart, your spirit, your mind,
They all will swell…

For you have taken a stand,
That you will not stand,
For what has been given to you on this earth,
As a man…
As a woman…
As a human being…
You will not go quietly,
Into that dark night,
You will not be taken silently…

Your blood may stain the sun on that day,
But you will never be taken away…
For on that day,

They will have to face,

The sound that will drown… This sound… Is what you will hear…

[def-uh-nish-uh n]

When the Levee breaks…

[def-uh-nish-uh n]

Six-Sided Die

"Six-Sided Die" describes how life is about choices. We live day to day, sometimes not realizing that we are slowly giving in to our own mortality. Life should never be about chance. We all only have one life to live. We should strive every day to be better than what we were the day before. The problem is that we get in the monotonous groove of life and allow ourselves to be halted from truly living. We all have a choice to live differently and to make our situations better. The problem is that we bet that life will bring us change rather than making the change ourselves. If you are unhappy with your life, try something different. Even if you make a wrong choice, you still have the choice to rectify your situation. Don't wait for something better…. Make it happen.

-Outlaw G

[def-uh-nish-uh n]

Six-Sided Die

When you hit rock bottom,
You will always land flat.
Your bones ache at the wake,
Of understanding these facts.

Life is about choice…

At some point,
You made the wrong one,
Now, you are gone from,
The life you once had,
It breaks you down even further,
From being mad,
To being sad.

You realize you're down so low…

Nothing in life is funny,
You're almost at the end of your rope,
You start asking for money,
Another realization is that everyday isn't sunny,
Because a dark cloud is overhead,
Your overhead,
Is over your head,
And you're way in over your head.

It shreds…

The little dignity you have left,
It makes you lose faith,
And you lose self-respect,
For yourself,
For your health,
It's a plague on your life,
It blinds your eyes to what's wrong,
And to also what's right.

There's no rest for the poor in spirit…
Soul crying out for more so that someone will hear it…

[def-uh-nish-uh n]

You wish you had more…

Time…

Money….

Anything of worth…

But you drown your sorrows in a bottle,
All the while you're still dying of thirst…

What makes things worse,
Is you can't hear the faint voice…
That's in the back of your mind saying…

"You still have a choice…"

When we fall,
It's a test of will,
To see who has the skill,
And to see who is built,

To survive…

Never bet your life on chance,

Life is not a six-sided die…

You have only one life to live…

You only have one life to give…

There's no rhyme or reason to why,

The choice you have to make,

Is to go on living…

Just living…

Or to truly be alive…

[def-uh-nish-uh n]

SELF-REFLECTION

"Self-Reflection" is a look into my own mind and how I have struggled with my own being. "Have I done enough? If tomorrow doesn't come for me, how will I be remembered? How can I do all these things? Where do I go from here?" These questions I ponder constantly. "Self-Reflection" is essentially putting these thoughts of doubt on paper in an attempt to convince myself what I am doing is the right thing to do. I am trying to encourage myself to not give in to the pressures of life, and not give up on the messages I am conveying. I consider myself a strong individual. Even strong people face their moments of doubt.

This self-reflection allows me to get a grip on my own life and push further.

-Outlaw G

[def-uh-nish-uh n]

SELF-REFLECTION

At times,

I ponder my purpose to live...

I have life...

I have light...

But what is it worth to give?

Is it better to be alive and not living?

Or to be gone from this world,
Having lead a life of giving?

I know,
I can't make it on my own,
I've lived a life at times where I've truly felt alone...

Forever rolling...

A rolling stone...

No place to rest my head,
No place to call home...

I fight my dreams on restless nights,
The nightmares of not living a fulfilled life,
Turning to the darkness and leaving the light,
Forgetting the difference of wrong and right...

I want to change the world,
Even if it means the destruction of my own,
What I fear most is what I do not know...

[def-uh-nish-uh n]

How much time do I have?
When will I be laid low?

How far can I go,
Before it's time to go?
I do not fear death,
I only fear what is left,
After I take my last breath,

What will be left?

I will give all my blood and sweat,
Tears and time,
To enlighten minds,
I must try…

Till the light inside,
Darkens and I'm without life,
I… Must… Strive…

I'll give it all to change,

For you… For me…

To be what I can…
To be who I am…

Supposed to be…

[def-uh-nish-uh n]

Put Back Together

"Put Back Together" is originally based off
another friend's piece of artwork. It was a
shattered vase that had been reconstructed by
the Japanese art of Kintsugi. Life has a way of
breaking us, leaving us shattered. Alex has
enhanced this idea with his sketch of a woman
who was broken but is slowly putting herself
back together. We can all learn from this style of
art. We can be put back together with time and
with care. If life should break you, know that
there are means to reconstruct your situation.
Through being put back together, we find
ourselves stronger and better for it. Never allow
yourself to remain broken. Let go of what has
happened. Start anew and begin life again
whole.

-Outlaw G

[def-uh-nish-uh n]

Put Back Together

We all fall apart,
Eventually…

It starts and then remains,
Continuously…

To slow our progress in life,
We regress,
In the mess,
That brings us strife…

It weighs on the mind,
It breaks up the being,
The waves of time crash,
To give you this feeling…

Of being broken,
Like life has been stolen…

It will remain a part of you,
To be apart from you,
As a blemish or a stain,
That can be cleansed,
It can be washed away…

Only if you mend,
And let that loss float away,
In those waves,
Of time,
You soon will find,
That being in pieces,
Will lead you to a ceaseless life of pain,
But through that rain,
Can you see what is precious?
It can put you back together,
It can bring breath to the breathless…

[def-uh-nish-uh n]

A sight to behold,
That leaves you left with nothing apart,
As a part,
Of you…

Gold to make yourself whole…
To make yourself refined and complete…
This gold…
Defined as glue…
For you…

To make yourself one…

Like Kintsugi…

[def-uh-nish-uh n]

Duality of Man (B E IN G)

The "Duality of Man" shows the two sides to my one mind. My real name is Evan and I have an alias, G. This shows the duality I have within me. Evan, or E, is the quiet, mild mannered, observant version of who I am. G, or Outlaw G, is the more outspoken, driven, and brash version of who I am. In my life I have found that I need to be both E and G. At times it can be difficult. I try to approach every situation with an objective outlook (E), but at times I find myself locked into a very subjective mind state (G). Not saying E is good and G is evil, but more so that E is passive and G is aggressive. I have relied on both sides in life, picking and choosing my battles accordingly. The problem that still looms is, can I be both at the same time? This to me is the perfect [Definition] of equilibrium that I strive for each day. Thus giving the term BEinG a whole different meaning.

-Outlaw G/Evan Geraci

[def-uh-nish-uh n]

THE DUALITY OF MAN (BEinG)

When you look into my eyes,
Tell me, what do you see?
Look past the black and blue,
And you will see me.

But who do you see? Which part of me?

Do you see the Outlaw rhyming G,
Or the ever mindful Evan, aka E?
And which one of these am I supposed to be?
I'm asking you because I don't know if I'm truly BEinG…

There are always two sides to every story,
One side is a downfall… The other is a road to glory.
One man's loss is another man's gain,
Where one empire falls…. Another takes its reign…

Without pain,
You can never really experience joy.
Through silence,
You can hear the loudest noise.
In darkness,
You can see the brightest light.
Sometimes being wrong,
Is better than doing wrong,
Because even being wrong,
Can still be right…

There are two sides to every coin,
Like there are two sides of every man,
Two faces in most cases,
Not many can understand…
Not many can comprehend,
What lies within,

[def-uh-nish-uh n]

Sometimes it's a conflict of the mind,
Sometimes it's a conflict to live.

E was the basis,
While G was in stasis,
G rose and awoke,
So that E could face this...
Life,
And strive truly for greatness,
Look deep into my eyes,
Hear my voice,
You will know I can't fake this...

I hope you're comprehending this composition of infliction,
On my brain that wains and weakens my position...
I'm just trying to be,
But its hard to explain because there's so much more to me.
There is a Jekyll and Hyde that lies deep inside,
Deep in my mind there is a great divide...

A vexed G,
An intellect E,
Shows you what grows inside of me...

One seeks Justice,
The other seeks Vengeance,
One rises above it,
The other sinks in it...

It's a war of attrition,
A walking contradiction...
Just a battle inside my mind,
An alarming condition...
But I do have a vision...
A perfect Definition...
Of what I am trying to be...
A Being,
More than just being...

I want to...

[def-uh-nish-uh n]

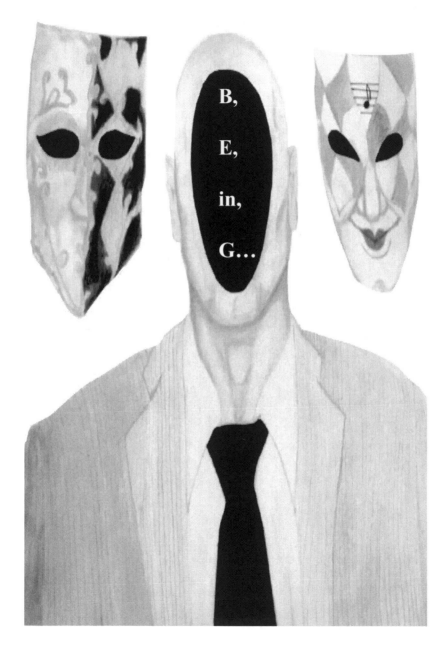

[def-uh-nish-uh n]

MARIGOLD

"Marigold" describes life from the perception of a flower. Though this flower is beautiful, it faces its own challenges to thrive. Weeds, oversaturated soil, not enough sunlight, all can hinder any flowers being. As in our own lives, we find ourselves to be cut off from what can truly help us grow. What Marigold is conveying is that we are all flowers in bloom. Some of us have fallen into situations in life that hinder us from growing. The key is never to give up hope in who you are. Your life is more precious than you realize. Never doubt yourself even when your situation looks bleak. The gardener we all seek to tend to us can represent different things to different people. Some believe their gardener is God or a variation of God. Some believe their gardener is their spouse, best friend, a family member, etc. It is always good to help out where we can. Sometimes help comes from unexpected places. Keep those who help you in mind. They may be helping you in more ways than one.

-Outlaw G

[def-uh-nish-uh n]

Marigold

Awake and realize,
Life's not what it could be,
You shake and epitomize,
A life you would never see…

Broken down,
Battered,
Body is withered,
Mind is scattered.
Your heart is now splintered…

The rain falls,
Feeling malnourished,
Soil is lose,
In it you won't flourish…

The foundation that you sprung from,
Is leaving you with questions and tiring conundrums…

"How can I grow, when my roots are loose?"

"How can I flourish, how can I produce?"

"How can I see the sun? I'm choked out by weeds,"

"They overshadow me, like the tallest of trees…"

"I can feel the rain, but in it I have no comfort,"

"I can't see it falling, I can only hear thunder,"

"I'm trapped, beneath this underbrush…"

"For if I am to survive, I have to do something,"

"I know I must…"

[def-uh-nish-uh n]

But what?

In life we find it hard at times to see the sun shine…

We all must keep hope so we can find that light…

Never give up hope to see a new day,
Don't worry about the weeds that stand in your way…

For you are a flower,
Almost in bloom,
You were planted by a hand,
That will tend to you soon,
Your gardener will not let your life slip away,
Your gardener will tend you,
Your life will be saved.

You will grow into something beautiful,
A sight to behold…

Strong…

Vibrant…

With a will of gold…

Though life at times,
May be shrouded,
And the skies above you,
May be clouded…

Know after the rain falls you will feel the sun…

To bask in…

To grow…

To make yourself one…

A flower in bloom…

[def-uh-nish-uh n]

<u>21</u>

"21" tells the story of an individual who has fallen prey to the dangers of gambling. It is not gambling itself that is wrong per se, instead betting all you have on chance can be. As stated in "Six-Sided Die," life should never be put to chance. I reference Kenny Rogers song "The Gambler" for emphasis on how life is not a game. The struggles we face in life can only be compounded when we bet what we have, and what we have saved on the luck of the draw. Be wary the next time you play Black Jack, you may be in for a turbulent time.

-Outlaw G

[def-uh-nish-uh n]

21

With a bad moon rising,
You start realizing,
How the end is drawing near.
The hour grows late,
It is a time of haste,
It is a time of ever growing fear…

Your fate…

Are strings pulled, then cut…

You stay… In your place,
But you know it is not enough…

Too late…

Your bet has been made,
You ponder your decisions on this game that you play…

You wait…

With anticipation,
Waiting for the end,
The cards that were dealt to you,
You hold and you bend…

For you lost your way, away from this seat,
Trying to make ends,
Trying to make amends,
For all of life's bad beats…

Out of luck…

Out of time…

Out of dimes…. It does not matter…

[def-uh-nish-uh n]

Blue on black…

Joker on jack…

Your life is now shattered…

Into pieces,
Your mind freezes,
The dealer makes his move,
To reveal to you,
That the hand dealt was ultimately doomed.

From the start,
You feel it in your heart,
As he flips his cards,
Your stomach sinks and you start to think,
"Why did I take it this far?"

"All I wanted was to take a chance and win."

"Never did I think I would lose again, and again."

"Gotta know when to hold 'em."

"Gotta know when to fold 'em."

"Guess I never learned that lesson."

"I should have done this… I should not have done that."

"This is what I get for betting."

A 21 stares you dead in the face,
You feel out of place…

Such distaste…

Such disgrace…

For all of your life had been taken away…

[def-uh-nish-uh n]

Everything you had…

Everything you've saved…

All taken away…

The cards read defeat,
Now with nothing left,
You must vacate your seat…

It's an easy squeeze on someone with greed,
On the mind to spend time,
Losing money with ease…

This may be your last time…

Sure hope you had fun…

But this is what you're up against…

When you face…

21…

[def-uh-nish-uh n]

DRIVE

"Drive" represents how we should all be driven to better ourselves and those around us. It is about establishing who you want to be as a person in society. Drive also describes that if your life is heading in the wrong direction, make a U turn and reroute. Learning to love who you are and where you are going in life will allow for your drive to be that much smoother. We all face bumpy roads from time to time. The key is to always look towards that open road to find our destination of being the best [Definition] of ourselves.

-Outlaw G

[def-uh-nish-uh n]

DRIVE

Life is more than just getting by,
There is a will to survive that lies deep inside,

Of you...

To be driven to drive,
There is more to you,
Than just being alive...

You have to be conditioned,
To harness your ambition,
Keep you eyes and ears open,
So you can listen.
Find your position,
To what you've been missing,
So in turn you can be the best [Definition],

Of you...

Even though you face immense pressure,
Don't base who you are on any false conjectures,
Rise above any demeaning lectures,
Become your own professor...

Teacher...

Leader...

Learn to accept,
That if your life is going in a different direction,
Intercept...

Redirect and inject yourself with love,

Kindness...

[def-uh-nish-uh n]

And self respect…

Learn compassion…

To seek passion…

It's an every day struggle and tussle,
But once you have it,

It is everlasting…

It will leave an impression,
On you and anyone around you,
They become a reflection,

Of you…

To give you stability and strength,
To where there is no question…

Within yourself you can find a solution,
To every problem you run into,

The key is to remain strong but constant with your movement…

Away from illusions…

Towards self-improvement…

Be the best you…

Be the very best [Definition] of you…

Each and every day remain true…

To you…

[def-uh-nish-uh n]

[def-uh-nish-uh n]

ENLIGHTENMENT

"Enlightenment" is based off a piece of artwork by Alex that shows Buddha sitting under a starry sky. This was the first piece of artwork, that Alex had made, that I created a piece for. I always found it fun to interpolate other artists pieces to create my own. "Enlightenment" is about achieving inner peace and seeing not just what is around you, but further on. Next time you look at the night sky to count the stars, look deeper into the vastness of space. In that darkness, you can find light that shines the brightest. Seek your own enlightenment.

-Outlaw G

[def-uh-nish-uh n]

ENLIGHTENMENT

To find enlightenment,
One must look to the stars to find the light in this,
World, and in this life,
Beyond all sight,
The stars collide,
In the night sky…

The stars in your mind,
You see through your third eye,
As thoughts materialize,
And you start to realize,
You are but a speck of sand,
A grain of rice…

In this life,
You make choices and sacrifices,
All toward a goal to find your road to be enlightened,
One must see,
But also be blind,
To know what is to come,
And know what to leave behind…

Your eyes can deceive you,
Your thoughts they can impede you,
But when you focus, they will never leave you…

Believe in you…

Believe you can find the nirvana of your mind,
What it is that you need,
That Inner peace,
A well so deep, in it,
Lies the enlightenment that you seek…

To light up the sky,
Open the third eye,
Break the mental binds,

Free… Your…

[def-uh-nish-uh n]

Mind...

[def-uh-nish-uh n]

From a Place

"From a Place" is a reference piece that describes my hometown of Louisville, Kentucky. The song "Mississippi" by David Banner is a major influence on this piece. I wanted to paint the picture of where I come from and how growing up in Louisville has impacted my life. This is my way of paying homage to sports hero's such as Muhammad Ali and Darrell Griffith, bring to light the floods the city has faced countless times, and to celebrate Thunder Over Louisville, the city's largest display of fireworks to kick off Derby Season. "From a Place" is to pay homage to my home. It is a place where I may no longer live, but I will cherish for the rest of my life.

-Outlaw G

[def-uh-nish-uh n]

From A Place

I'm from a place…

Where thoroughbreds race in the mud,
Where you crack a ball on a bat,
And catch it in a glove.
Where the bourbon flows,
Wheat and rye,
Where the bluegrass grows,
Where the cardinals fly…

I'm from a place…

Home of Dr. Dunkenstein,
Who mesmerized every eye,
When he soared through the air,
To hang our banners high…

I'm from a place…

Where the waters would rise,
But always subside,
Where we build and revive,
Our homes and our lives…

I'm from a place…

Where the arts are the spark,
Where the future has a start,
Where we all play our parts,
With love in our hearts…

I'm from a place…

Where before every summer,
We hear a loud thunder,
Over the river, every year… It is a magnificent wonder…

[def-uh-nish-uh n]

I'm from a place…

Where a butterfly stung like a bee,
A man who was molded as Clay,
But grew to be the greatest, his name, Ali.
A world champ three times,
He could never be stopped,
Jab,
Jab,
Right cross,
Leaving every opponent rocked,

I'm from a place…

Where I truly call home,
Where I can go when I'm old,
And never feel alone.

I'm from a place where I truly belong,
I'm from a place that forever makes me strong.

I'm from a place…

Louisville…

Home…

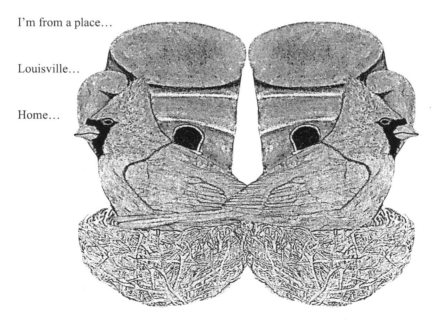

[def-uh-nish-uh n]

I CARE G

My name is Evan Geraci. I love my name. I love what it represents. "I Care G" is showing how proud I am to be who I am. It is also a thank you to anyone and everyone who has ever cared for me or cared about me. When I began writing this book I said to myself, "There is more to my name than meets the eye." So I decided to play around with how Geraci is spelled. I Care G is the embodiment of who I am and how I want the world to see me. Reading this now, you might not quite understand, but I hope, in time, you will. I thank you for going on this journey with me and experiencing life how I see it. I will continue to be the BEinG I am striving to be. I have one final piece of advice: through all the pitfalls, potholes, brick walls and obstacles…

Always be the best [Definition] of yourself.

-Outlaw G

[def-uh-nish-uh n]

I CARE G

An age old question, what's really to name?
Some misuse it,
Some abuse it,
For a little speck of fame...

My name,
Has a much deeper meaning,
It derives and exemplifies,
A much deeper feeling...

Geraci,
It comes from the island of Sicily,
I take pride in the pride it gives me,
But I want to describe it visually.

Geraci...

With it,
I feel the warmth of the sun
And I embrace the cool breeze,
I'm ever mindful
And I get an eyeful,
Of the world that lies beneath me.
I am a hawk,
A bird of prey,
I soar through the sky,
Flying towards the horizon,
Flying free...
Flying high...

Look deeper, tell me,
What's in a name?
From it, tell me,
What can you gain?
There is more to explore,
To you I implore, It is more than simple and plain...

[def-uh-nish-uh n]

Geraci…

G is for the Good, that I try to convey,
E is for Everyone, I meet on my way,
R is for Respect, that I give and I show,
A is for All, that have helped me grow,
C Is for the Constant strive to be more,
I is for I love you, words to live and die for…

Even with this,
there is much more to be gained,
Of how a name is more,
Than simple and plain…

Let's take this same name,
And spell it out in reverse,
Let's look at it a different way,
To see how much more we can learn…

I,

C,

A,

R,

E,

G,

Meaning,
I care for those,
Who have always cared,
For me…
I care, G…
I care who you are,
How you conduct yourself,
I care for your self worth,
I care for your health…

[def-uh-nish-uh n]

Honestly I might care,
Just a little too much,
But If I care,
It's my burden to bare,
Then that means I care,
Enough.

I care,
G...
Those words I hold true,
But I care G,
Means you care for me too...

That means,
If I have "The Weight" on my chest,
And the world puts me to the test,
Or "The Levee" won't break,
and I have nothing left...
You put all to rest,
And allow me to rest,
So I can strive,
To survive this life,
And be my very best...

That means if I live my life,
On a "Six-Sided Die..."
Leaving life to chance,
You will give me an injection
Of "Self-Reflection,"
So I can regain,
My steadfast stance...
That means you will put me "Back Together,"
Like a carpenter's hands,
Allow me,
To B E in G
"As the Duality of Man...."
That means you will tend to me,
Like a "Marigold,"
Not let the "21" leave me undone,
Instead keep me whole...

[def-uh-nish-uh n]

That means you will "Drive" through this life,
At the same time keep me driven,
Towards "Enlightenment,"
I desire this,
To be the perfect [Definition]…

That means you understand "I'm From A Place,"
Even though I'm far from home,
I Care G means,
I will never feel alone…

So take these words in,
From them you have much you can gain,
There is always more to me,
There is always more to my name

It is more than simple and plain…

It is my name…

GERACI = I CARE G

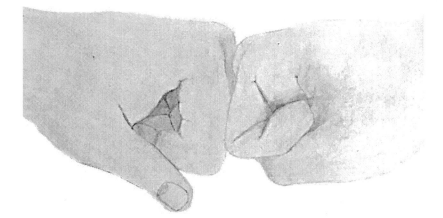

[def-uh-nish-uh n]